12 STORIES ABOUT **HELPING THE COMMUNITY**

by Samantha S. Bell

STORY LIBRARY

MORE TO EXPLORE

www.12StoryLibrary.com

12-Story Library is an imprint of Bookstaves.

Photographs ©: sirtravelalot/Shutterstock.com, cover, 1; Habitat for Humanity International/PD, 4; Delta New Hub/CC2.0, 4; Kathy Hutchins/Shutterstock.com, 5; Sgt. Summer Woode/US Army, 6; Consumers Energy/CC2.0, 7; FoodBankCENC.org/CC2.0, 8; New Africa/Shutterstock.com, 9; Mike Mozart/CC2.0, 9; Sodexo USA/CC2.0, 10; US Army Corps of Engineers/Sara Corbett, 11; Rawpixel.com/Shutterstock.com, 11; gpointstudio/Shutterstock.com, 12; stockfour/Shutterstock.com, 13; National Main Street Center, Inc./YouTube, 14; Kenneth Sponsler/Shutterstock.com, 14; Monkey Business Images/Shutterstock.com, 15; Kathy Hutchins/Shutterstock.com, 16; From One Hand to Another/YouTube, 17; Jose Luis Carrascosa/Shutterstock.com, 18; Rob Crandall/Shutterstock.com, 19; Rawpixel.com/Shutterstock.com, 20; United Way of America/PD, 20; Tharun 15/Shutterstock.com, 21; Africa Studio/Shutterstock.com, 21; Terry Grahl/YouTube, 22; Terry Grahl/YouTube, 23; NJTV News/YouTube, 24; Mrsitchathome/CC4.0, 25; Toys for Tots/PD, 26; US Embassy/PD, 26; US Navy, 27; Corey Lewis/US Navy, 28; Rawpixel.com/Shutterstock.com, 29

ISBN
9781632357434 (hardcover)
9781632358523 (paperback)
9781645820284 (ebook)

Library of Congress Control Number: 2019938685

Printed in the United States of America
October 2019

About the Cover

A family works in a community garden.

Access free, up-to-date content on this topic plus a full digital version of this book. Scan the QR code on page 31 or use your school's login at 12StoryLibrary.com.

Table of Contents

Habitat for Humanity: Putting People in Homes of Their Own.... 4

Big Brothers Big Sisters: Building Relationships 6

Bank of America: Finding Ways to Give Back 8

Katie's Krops: Fighting Hunger with Healthy Food 10

Dress for Success: Helping Women Find Confidence and Jobs ... 12

National Main Street Center: Bringing Downtowns Back to Life.. 14

Pharrell Williams and FOHTA: Free STEAMM for Kids 16

Carpool Vote: Getting People to the Polls 18

United Way: Helping Communities Help Themselves 20

Enchanted Makeovers: Bringing Hope to Women and Children . 22

Angel Flight Northeast: Taking Patients Where They Need to Go. 24

Marine Toys for Tots: Bringing Holiday Cheer 26

Ways You Can Help.. 28

Glossary 30

Read More 31

Index.. 32

About the Author 32

1 Habitat for Humanity: Putting People in Homes of Their Own

To buy a home, people usually save money to use as a down payment. But sometimes that's hard to do. They may not earn much money. They may have medical bills to pay. They may have lost their jobs. Some people think they will never be able to buy a home. That's when Habitat for Humanity steps in to help.

Habitat believes everyone should have a safe, decent, affordable home. The global nonprofit helps people in need get homes of their own. Men, women, and teens in the community volunteer to renovate or build the houses. The people who will live in the houses work hard, too. They help build their homes. They learn new skills. They take classes to find out how to budget

and handle money. They learn how to keep up a home. They volunteer at Habitat's home improvement store and other community projects.

Habitat for Humanity was founded by Millard and Linda Fuller in 1976.

Today the organization works in 1,400 communities across the United States and 70 countries around the world. It has helped more than 13 million people build or improve homes of their own.

TRIPLEXES FOR TEACHERS

In 2019, the school district in Big Sky, Montana, teamed up with Habitat for Humanity. Housing in the area is very expensive. Teachers are having a hard time finding places to live. The district decided to build triplexes on school property. Habitat for Humanity will help build them. The triplexes will be affordable housing for teachers.

15 months

Minimum time it takes to build a Habitat house

- Habitat loans the people the money to buy their home.
- The people do not have to pay any interest on the loan.
- The amount of the payments is based on how much the people earn.

2 Big Brothers Big Sisters: Building Relationships

Big Sister Summer and little sister Stephanie enjoy skating when they get together.

5

Years old a child must be to join the program

- In BBBS, the adult mentors are called Bigs.
- The young people are known as Littles.
- Many boys and girls are on waiting lists for mentors.

Big Brothers Big Sisters (BBBS) began in 1904. This organization helps teenagers and children who are facing hardships and challenges in their lives. They may be struggling in school or heading for trouble. BBBS wants to help them make good choices and be successful.

BBBS matches the young people with adult volunteers. The adults are called mentors. "Mentor" is a word that means "trusted advisor." Female mentors are matched with girls, and male mentors are matched with boys. The young people and the adults spend one-on-one time together. They might meet every week or every other week. They might go out to eat or see a movie. They might play games, shoot hoops, or visit a zoo or museum. Over time, they get to know each other.

The mentors support the young people in many different ways. They listen to their problems and help them through difficult times. They cheer the students on as they work toward their goals. They help them gain more confidence. The mentors and students build strong relationships. Some last for many years, long after the students have become adults.

BIGS IN BUSINESSS

Sometimes adults want to volunteer for BBBS, but they don't have a lot of time. To solve this problem, some areas have started programs called Bigs in Business. Adults volunteer as mentors. But instead of doing activities in the evenings or on weekends, they meet their littles during the workday. Middle school and high school students ride a bus to visit their Bigs at work.

3

Bank of America: Finding Ways to Give Back

Some companies give back to their communities. They know that strong communities help businesses grow. Bank of America helps communities in many different ways. One way is by raising money. The company gives the money to charities and nonprofit groups that meet people's needs. These include home building programs and food banks. In 2017, Bank of America gave nearly $800,000 to charities in Nashville, Tennessee, alone.

The company encourages their employees to give back, too. If an employee wants to donate money to a charity, Bank of America will give the same amount. Employees are also encouraged to volunteer. In 2016, more than 54,000 Bank of America employees volunteered in their communities. Some worked as mentors for young people. Others helped build houses. Employees can even get time off work to volunteer.

Bank of America volunteers help out at their local food shelf.

2 million

Number of hours Bank of America employees volunteered in 2017

- They worked through the company's social responsibility program.
- In 2014, Bank of America started a Global Volunteer Awards program to recognize employees for outstanding commitment to their communities.
- Award winners can choose a charity to receive a special donation from the company.

Sometimes employees volunteer as a group. In 2019, 50 Bank of America employees got together to pack bags of food. The food was given to schoolchildren whose families don't have much money. The children took the food home to have something to eat over the weekend.

Bank of America also created the Neighborhood Builder program to help nonprofit organizations. Besides providing money, the program trains the leaders. It helps the groups become stronger. Then they can serve their communities better.

4 Katie's Krops: Fighting Hunger with Healthy Food

In 2008, Katie Stagliano received a cabbage seedling as part of a program at her school. She was in third grade. Katie and her brother planted the seedling in their backyard. Her cabbage grew and grew. Eventually it weighed 40 pounds (18 kg).

Katie wanted to do something special with her huge cabbage. She decided to give it to people who were hungry. Katie and her family took the cabbage to a local soup kitchen. She helped serve the cabbage to the people who came.

From then on, Katie wanted to help provide healthy food for the hungry. She planted a vegetable garden. She donated the vegetables to people in need. But she wanted to do more.

Katie started Katie's Krops to encourage young people to fight hunger through gardening. Children and youth plant vegetable gardens. Then they donate their harvest to soup kitchens, homeless shelters, and food banks. Katie's Krops supplies them with everything they need to have a successful garden. By 2018, Katie's Krops had helped establish 100 gardens in more than 30 states.

AWARD-WINNING WORK

Katie has received several awards for her work. The American Horticultural Society presented her with the Jane L. Taylor Award. This award recognizes individuals who encourage children to garden. In 2012, Katie was the youngest person to receive the Clinton Global Citizen Award for Leadership in Civil Society. She also received the Joseph P. Riley Jr. Vision Award for being a model citizen.

275

Number of people who ate Katie's cabbage

- Katie's Krops sponsors a free summer camp.
- About 10 Katie's Krops growers are invited to attend.
- The campers learn new growing techniques and work on service projects.

5 Dress for Success: Helping Women Find Confidence and Jobs

When someone is looking for a job, they usually go to job interviews. It's important to appear neat and professional. If people wear the wrong type of clothing to an interview, they may not get the job. But some people can't afford to buy new clothes.

Low-income women who need clothes for interviews or work can go to Dress for Success. The

1 million+

Number of women who have been served by Dress for Success

- A law student named Nancy Lublin started Dress for Success in 1997.
- She began with a $5,000 inheritance from her great-grandfather.
- Her organization now has 155 offices in 29 countries. There are more than 12,000 volunteers.

Dress for Success helps women meet the challenges of interviewing for a new job.

organization provides professional clothes for free. Women can choose from racks of dresses and blazers. They can also pick out accessories such as jewelry and purses. When a woman has the right clothes for an interview, she has more confidence.

Dress for Success supports women in other ways. Volunteers help them write their résumés and cover letters. They guide them through practice interviews. This way, the women know what to expect. They learn to speak clearly and express themselves well. When they go to an interview, they look and sound professional.

Some women can't make it to the Dress for Success locations. So the organization has created mobile units. These travel to different areas with clothes, shoes, and other items the women may need.

THINK ABOUT IT

Have you ever dressed up for a special celebration or event? How did you feel? Do you think you would have felt the same in your everyday clothes?

6 National Main Street Center: Bringing Downtowns Back to Life

In many cities, the downtown areas are doing well. Businesses are thriving. New businesses are starting up or moving in. Locals and visitors shop in the stores and eat in the restaurants. Arts and culture events draw crowds. These downtowns are places where people live, work, and play. They like being there. They feel they belong.

But some downtowns are struggling. Stores and businesses have shut down or moved away. Jobs have disappeared. Buildings are vacant. Streets are empty. There's nothing to see or do. These places don't seem to have much of a future.

The National Main Street Center is helping these areas come back to life. Through a program called Main Street America, it shares knowledge

MAIN STREET AMERICA™

Main Street America helps bring the community together to make their downtowns strong again.

and information with community leaders. The leaders learn ways to make their downtowns strong again.

2,000+

Number of neighborhoods and communities the National Main Street Center has helped

- The organization was started in 1980. Its main office is in Chicago.
- Many downtowns today are busy, lively places because of the National Main Street Center.
- Each year, the National Main Street Center gives the Great American Main Street Award (GAMSA) to at least three communities. For them, the future looks bright.

One way is to fix up older, historic buildings instead of knocking them down. These buildings give a place character. They are also part of a community's history. Another way is to invest in small local businesses. These create jobs and make the economy stronger.

Vacant buildings can be turned into cool living spaces. Wider sidewalks can make downtowns more walkable. Leaders learn how to get community members involved. They learn why arts and culture are important. Through Main Street America, they connect with other leaders across the country. They share ideas and solutions. Experts from Main Street America give advice. They check on how communities are doing.

7

Pharrell Williams and FOHTA: Free STEAMM for Kids

Pharrell Williams is many things. He is a rapper, singer, and songwriter.

From One Hand To AnOTHER

He is a record producer and fashion designer. He is also someone who cares about kids. Williams has performed around the world. When he began traveling, he was exposed to different cultures and ways of thinking. He realized that many other people don't have these opportunities. He wanted to give kids new learning experiences that would help them succeed in life. When he was growing up, his teachers encouraged him to use his talents. Williams wants to encourage kids today to use their gifts.

In 2008, Williams started FOHTA. This stands for From One Hand To Another. Each summer, FOHTA holds summer camps for elementary and middle school students. Most of the students are at-risk or low-income kids. The camps focus on STEAMM. This stands for Science, Technology, Engineering, Arts, Mathematics, and Motivation. Students do science experiments and learn computer

Students performing at a FOHTA camp in 2017.

HANDS-ON MEDICINE

In 2018, professors, residents, and students from East Virginia Medical Center led some of the FOHTA camp programs. Campers learned how to tie a tourniquet. They saw how ultrasounds work. They learned how to stop a wound from bleeding. The school wanted campers to know about some of the opportunities in the medical field.

coding. They take classes in foreign languages. They dance, make art, and do yoga.

Williams wants students to enjoy learning. He wants to help them find their passions and achieve their dreams. More than 1,700 kids attend FOHTA camps each summer. The camps are free of charge for the families.

6

Number of weeks a FOHTA summer camp lasts

- Schools and organizations in the community provide programs for the camps.
- Pharrell Williams wants the camps to create curiosity in kids.
- Breakfast and lunch are served every day.

8

Carpool Vote: Getting People to the Polls

Carpool Vote volunteers drive people to and from the polls.

Every American citizen 18 or older has the right to vote. During elections, people must go to polling places to vote. But some have trouble getting there. They may not have a car or enough money for gasoline. They may not be able to drive. They may not have access to public transportation. Carpool Vote helps people get to the polls.

People visit the Carpool Vote website or dial a number to request a ride. They can also make special requests. For example, elderly voters may want a friend or family member to go with them. They can request an extra seat in the car.

The drivers are volunteers. Carpool Vote's system matches riders with drivers. Drivers contact the voters by email, phone, or text. Then they pick up voters, take them to the polls, wait while they vote, and drop them off at home again.

THINK ABOUT IT

Elections are supposed to show officials how people feel about the issues. But when people can't vote, their voices aren't heard. How do you think this affects the election?

Carpool Vote is not connected with any political party. Drivers are not allowed to wear campaign hats or T-shirts or talk about the issues. It doesn't matter which candidates riders will vote for. What matters is that everyone uses their right to vote.

2016

Year when Carpool Vote began

- Many young people and elderly people have trouble getting to the polls.
- People of color and people with disabilities often need rides, too.
- Carpool Vote also helps people get photo IDs, a requirement for voting in some states.

9

United Way: Helping Communities Help Themselves

United Way knows that for people to live well, they need three things. They need an education that leads to a good job. They need the resources to be healthy. And they need enough money to meet their basic needs for food, shelter, and safety. When people are missing any of these, they may experience some hard times. United Way shows people how to reach out and help others in their community.

Every community is different. Because of this, every United Way group is different. Each has its own goals for its own community. The groups are led by volunteers, and volunteers do the work.

There are many ways people can volunteer. Some help raise money for improvements in the community. Others tutor schoolchildren or help adults learn to read. They might improve a park or rebuild a community center. They can help organize support groups for people dealing with certain diseases. They can pick up litter. They can become part of a program to protect local wildlife. There's a way for every volunteer to help.

Children and youth can be volunteers, too. There is even a special event for young volunteers. Every year, young people ages 5 to 25 can participate in Global Youth Service Day (GYSD). The event brings together more than 800 organizations, including United Way groups. They work together to make their communities stronger.

1,800+

Number of communities around the world where United Way works

- There are United Way agencies in 40 countries.
- United Way began in Denver, Colorado, in 1887. It was called the Charity Organization Society.
- It raised $21,700 in its first fundraiser.

10

Enchanted Makeovers: Bringing Hope to Women and Children

Terry Grahl had an interior design business in Michigan. Then someone asked her to paint a wall in a local shelter. Women and children lived at the shelter. Some had been abused. Others had nowhere else to go.

Grahl went to see the shelter. The walls were plain and drab. The beds came from a prison. The mattresses and bedspreads were old and worn. The shelter had a good program, but the living area did not give women and children any hope.

Grahl did more than paint a wall. She brought in artists to paint murals. People donated new beds and replaced the carpet. The rooms became colorful and cheery. Grahl

decided to close her business and start a new organization. She called it Enchanted Makeovers.

Enchanted Makeovers uses many handmade items when renovating a shelter. Volunteers make curtains, quilts, and blankets. They also make pillowcases and dolls the residents can keep. For some, these are the first handmade gifts they have ever received. Enchanted Makeovers wants the residents to feel valuable and loved.

Enchanted Makeovers now works to change shelters across the country. The new living spaces they create help bring healing and encouragement to the residents.

2007
Year when Enchanted Makeovers began

- Volunteers sew capes for the children, too.
- The capes help the children feel like superheroes.
- They inspire creativity and positive thinking.

SACRED SEWING

Some shelters with Enchanted Makeovers have a special room for sewing. Grahl calls these Sacred Sewing Rooms. Like the rest of the shelter, the rooms are cheerful. They are full of sewing machines, fabric, and patterns. If the women don't know how to sew, they can learn. Sewing helps many women cope with their problems. They can also make items to give to others in need.

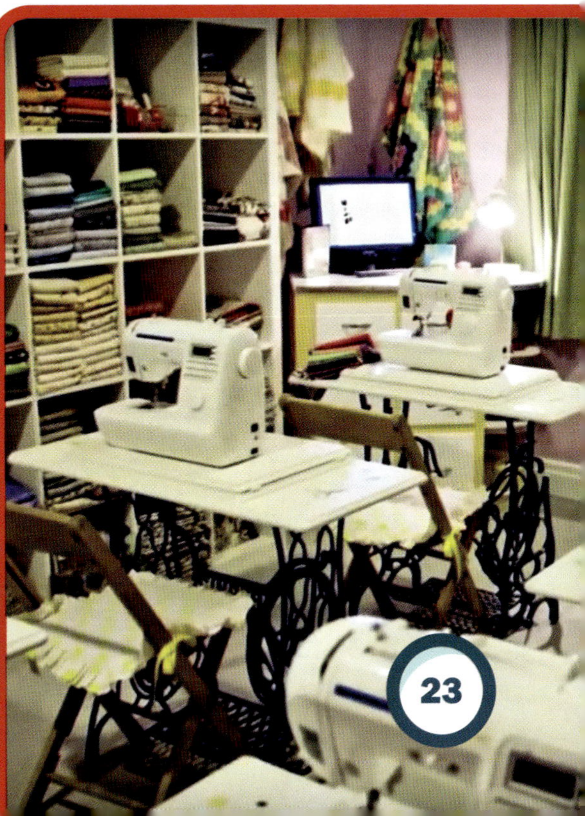

11

Angel Flight Northeast: Taking Patients Where They Need to Go

Sometimes people have to travel long distances for medical care. But traveling can be difficult for the patient. A car ride may take several hours. The fastest way to go is by airplane. But flying can be very expensive. The patient might be too sick to travel in a commercial plane. If the patient lives in the northeastern United States, Angel Flight Northeast (NE) steps in to help.

Larry Camerlin in 2015.

$300

Approximate cost of each Angel Flight

- From 1996 to 2018, more than 74,000 patients used Angel Flight NE.
- Angel Flight NE also has a partnership with some commercial airlines.
- The airlines provide seats for Angel Flight patients when the distance is too far or the weather is bad.

More than 1,000 pilots are part of Angel Flight NE. They use their personal airplanes to fly patients and their families from one city to another. The pilots are volunteers. The families don't have to pay for the trip, fuel, or other flight expenses.

ANGELS ON THE GROUND

Even people who aren't pilots can get involved in Angel Flight NE. Some volunteers are called Earth Angels. They drive patients from airports to hospitals and other places for medical care. Earth Angels are often the first people patients see after their appointments. If the patients received bad news, the Earth Angels are there to comfort them.

Angel Flight organizations are found throughout the United States. Angel Flight NE was started in 1996 by Larry Camerlin, a pilot and a former priest. He used to have an ambulance business. He also enjoyed flying. Camerlin decided to combine the two to help patients in New England.

The pilots are all ages. Some are doctors or lawyers. Others are retired. But they all love to fly and they want to help someone. They never limit the number of flights a patient can take. They will fly people as far and as often as they need.

12

Marine Toys for Tots: Bringing Holiday Cheer

In 1947, Diane Hendricks created a few handmade dolls. She asked her husband Bill to take them to a local agency. She wanted to give them to children in need.

Bill was a major in the United States Marine Corps Reserve. He could not find an agency that would take the dolls, so he started one. The other marines in his unit joined him. They collected and gave away 5,000 toys that year. Marine Toys for Tots had begun. In 1948, the US Marine Corps made it a nationwide community action project. Marines at reserve centers all over the country collected and handed out toys.

Today Toys for Tots gives away more than 18 million toys each year. They give them to less fortunate children at Christmastime. They want to bring the children joy and hope during the holiday season.

Drop-off boxes are placed around cities and towns. People bring new, unwrapped toys and place them in the boxes. They also donate books, clothes, and games. Parents can come on distribution days and pick out items for their children. Many of the parents could not afford to buy presents. They feel good that they can give their children Christmas gifts.

Former First Lady Michelle Obama helps with a Toys for Tots drive in 2015.

7 million

Approximate number of children who receive toys each year

- In September 2017, Hurricane Maria destroyed many homes in Puerto Rico.
- At Christmastime, Toys for Tots worked with Hasbro Toy Company to bring toys to children there.
- In December, they delivered more than 30,000 toys.

THINK ABOUT IT

Major Hendricks started Toys for Tots because he saw a need in his community. Find a need in your community. What can you do to help?

The gifts are not just for young children. Teenagers also receive gifts from Toys for Tots. These include sports balls and craft kits. People donate items like purses, headphones, and makeup kits.

Ways You Can Help

- Make cards or gifts for children in the hospital.
- Go to a local nursing home and visit with the residents. You can play games, perform on an instrument, sing, or just tell them about your day.
- Join in a charity fundraiser, such as a 5K run.
- Help an elderly neighbor with yard work. Plant flowers, mow the lawn, blow leaves, or pull weeds.
- Write a letter or draw a picture to thank a soldier for his or her service.
- Go to a local homeless shelter with your family to help cook, set the tables, or serve meals.
- Be a mother's helper for a mom with a new baby.

- Organize a canned food drive in your neighborhood. Take the cans to a local food shelf or pantry.

- Participate in Global Youth Service Day. Ask an adult for help in getting started.

- Start a Katie's Krops garden. Visit katieskrops.com on the web to find out how.

Glossary

charity
An organization that gives aid to people in need.

down payment
The first payment made when borrowing money to buy a house.

interview
A meeting between a worker and employer to see if the worker is a good fit for the business.

interior design
The art of decorating the rooms in a building.

mural
A painting on a wall.

nonprofit
An organization that does not make a profit from their work. It uses the money it earns or raises to do its work and run the organization.

résumé
A document listing a person's job experience and qualifications.

renovate
To make something new again.

soup kitchen
A place where free food is served to homeless people.

tourniquet
A device used to stop or slow the blood flow from a wound.

triplex
An apartment with three floors.

ultrasound
A medical technique that uses ultrasonic vibrations to create images of things inside the body.

Read More

Andres, Marco. *Community Service and Volunteering.* New York: PowerKids Press, 2018.

Andrus, Aubre. *101 Small Ways to Change the World.* Oakland, CA: Lonely Planet Kids, 2018.

Paul, Caroline. *You Are Mighty: A Guide to Changing the World.* New York: Bloomsbury Children's Books, 2018.

Stagliano, Katie. *Katie's Cabbage.* Young Palmetto Books. Columbia, SC: University of South Carolina Press, 2015.

Index

affordable housing, 4-5
Angel Flight Northeast, 24-25

Bank of America, 8-9
Big Brothers Big Sisters (BBBS), 6-7

Camerlin, Larry, 24-25
Carpool Vote, 18-19
creating jobs, 15

Dress for Success, 12-13
driving voters, 18-19

Enchanted Makeovers, 22-23

facing hardships, kids, 6-7
flying patients, 24-25
food for the hungry, 8-9, 10-11, 20, 29
From One Hand To Another (FOHTA), 16-17

gardening, 10-11
gifts for children, 26-27
giving money, 8-9
Grahl, Terry, 22-23

Habitat for Humanity, 4-5
helping shelters, 22-23, 28

job help, 12-13
Katie's Krops, 10-11, 29

Main Street America, 14-15
mentoring, 6-7

supporting communities, 14-15, 20-21

teaching at-risk kids, 16-17
Toys for Tots, 26-27

United Way, 20-21

volunteering, 4, 6-7, 8-9, 13, 18, 20-21, 23, 24-25

ways to help, 28-29
Williams, Pharrell, 16-17

About the Author

Samantha S. Bell lives in upstate South Carolina with her family and lots of animals. She is the author of more than 100 nonfiction books for children.